Dazzle Like Dolly

Dazzle Like Dolly

Games, Activities, Quizzes & Fun Inspired by the Queen of Country

Jessica MacLeish

HARPER

An Imprint of HarperCollinsPublishers

ISBN 978-0-06-327052-7

Typography by Jessica Nordskog

COS

First Edition

To all the
Dollys out there:
may you always
shine bright
and be *you!*

"A rhinestone shines as good as a diamond."

Nobody lives life to the fullest like musical genius, cultural icon, and everyone's favorite human: Dolly Parton!

Dolly does it all—writes songs, sings, plays musical instruments, runs her own businesses, gives back to her community and communities all over the world, speaks her mind, and spends time with her family and friends. *Whew!* And through it all, she shines bright like the special gemstone she is.

WHAT HAS DOLLY DONE?

 launched ventures like her Netflix shows and perfumes

 works on other writing projects, such as her novel with James Patterson: *Run, Rose, Run*

 runs the business of her music and Dollywood, her amusement park

 leads philanthropic initiatives like her Imagination Library and more

But even more important than *what Dolly does* is *who Dolly is.* She's *more* than her accomplishments, after all. Dolly is true to herself, welcoming and helpful to others, and gets more creative with each passing day. These are just *some* of the qualities that make her so beloved by almost everyone—moms, dads, kids, grandparents . . . people from every which way and every walk of life come together in their admiration of Dolly and her music. That's pretty special.

Dolly's can-do attitude toward life brings people together—and it's something we all can learn from, in good times and bad. Whether we've just won the big game, gotten a great grade, made a new friend or are dealing with a friendship ending, frustrated by a setback, or just feeling overwhelmed, we can look to Dolly's life to find guidance and inspiration.

So what would Dolly do in those situations and others, and how can *you* channel *your* inner Dolly to sparkle a little brighter in your own life?

Keep reading (something Dolly *loves* to do, btw)! By the end of this book, you'll be walking the Dolly walk, talking the Dolly talk, and shining in a way that only *you* can shine—just like Dolly does!

Dreamin' Big and *Workin'* Hard

Did you know that Dolly Parton dreamed of becoming a famous musician when she was a little girl growing up in rural Tennessee? Did you also know that believing in herself—despite the odds against her—is one of the many things Dolly did to make her dream come true? Well, now you do.

After visiting Cas Walker's *Farm and Home Hour*, a popular variety show in Knoxville, on a class trip, Dolly felt she was destined to sing on that show. (She'd loved music and singing *forever*—but when she saw Cas's show, she instantly knew her life's calling!) But how could a girl with dirt under her nails ever get up onstage, much less be a superstar? Dolly didn't know how she'd do it, but she knew she belonged in the music world. She just had to find a way to make it happen!

When she was just ten years old, Dolly got backstage at Cas's radio show and managed to talk her way into her big break—singing on his show! This was her chance to prove herself. And the crowd cheered for her so loud, she had to do an encore.

That performance was a huge confidence booster for

Dolly. She wasn't the only one who believed that she could become a music star. People really seemed to like her singing.

When she graduated from high school, all her classmates stood up to share what they planned to do next. Dolly wasn't afraid to speak her truth: "I'm going to Nashville, and I'm gonna be a star."

They all laughed at her! And that was embarrassing enough to make Dolly blush, but it didn't stop her from chasing her dreams. Nothing could ever stop Dolly from chasing her dreams.

Okay, time to spill. What are some of your wildest dreams? Think *big*, as big as Dolly's hair is at its most done up.

Use this space to brainstorm some bold, daring dreams you can go after. (For example, maybe a dream of yours is to perform onstage with Dolly herself one day! Never say never.)

Then think about a few steps you can take to turn your dreams into reality. What can you do now to get started?

Make a list of goals that will put you on that path. What do you want to accomplish today? This week? This month? This year?

What about the next five years and beyond?

Breaking your big dreams down into small steps is a tried-and-true strategy for building the life you dream of. Success doesn't happen overnight, y'know. Even Dolly didn't become a chart-topping songstress in one day!

BRAINSTORM YOUR DREAMS

WRITE YOUR GOALS

Dolly knows better than anyone that good fortune isn't handed to you—you gotta work for it with a little sweat and elbow grease.

One of the first things Dolly did when she set her sights on becoming a musician was to learn to play different instruments. She devoted all her time and energy to mastering her craft. She taught herself how to play and kept at it, no matter how hard it seemed.

Inside every one of us is the grit and perseverance that Dolly is known for. You can turn your passion into action to make your dreams come true. Got it? Good!

WHAT CAN DOLLY PLAY?

dulcimer	banjo	recorder
Autoharp	guitar	violin
electric guitar	piano	fiddle
pan flute	mandolin	harmonica
	saxophone	

Yes, really, all of these!

Just remember:

"**You're not going to see your dreams come true if you don't put wings, legs, arms, hands, and feet on 'em.**"

"I have looked up at a glass ceiling and thrown one of my five-inch heels and smashed right through it."

Dreaming big and working hard to achieve those dreams is the Dolly Parton special. Here are just a *few* examples of how hard Dolly has worked along the way:

 Dolly never liked school (though she loved to read from a young age), but she was determined to be the first in her family to finish high school, just to prove she could.

 When Dolly was asked to write fifteen songs for a Broadway musical version of *9 to 5*, she wrote thirty.

 When Dolly landed her first film role in *9 to 5*, she showed up to the set with the whole script memorized—not just her own lines! She also wrote (and sang) the theme song for the movie, which became a huge No. 1 hit.

 For her role as a hairdresser in the movie *Steel Magnolias*, Dolly learned how to cut and style hair for real.

Dolly Parton has never been afraid of a little (or a lot of) hard work, and there's no need for you to be, either. As Dolly says, "If you're gonna make a dream come true, you gotta work it."

What are some ways you could give a little extra—like Dolly often does—on something you're working hard at? Could you do extra credit on a homework assignment? Practice your instrument an extra hour each week?

LIST YOUR IDEAS HERE:

_____

_____

_____

_____

_____

_____

_____

_____

_____

_____

_____
_____
_____
_____
_____
_____
_____
_____

And how can doing a little extra help you achieve your dream?

_____
_____
_____
_____
_____
_____

One thing that can help when it comes time to get to work? Good music, of course.

Whether you're writing it, singing it, or just listening to it, some good tunes can inspire you to get into the work zone and give you the energy to go that extra mile. And hey, working with a soundtrack is more fun than working without one!

Go on and make yourself a working-hard playlist that you can listen to whenever you need to buckle down and get some work done.

Here's the perfect Dolly track to help you get your playlist started:

"9 to 5" by Dolly Parton

_____
_____
_____
_____
_____
_____
_____
_____
_____
_____
_____
_____
_____
_____
_____

"You've gotta have people to help carry out those dreams . . ."

Ask Dolly and she'd probably tell you that hard work doesn't have to be a solo activity. Your dreams and accomplishments will always be all your own but asking for and accepting the help of friends or family is important, too. You can accomplish even more—maybe bigger and better things—when you have a great partner or team.

Don't forget that you can always ask for a helping hand— even Dolly Parton asks for help when she needs it.

WHO'S HELPED DOLLY OUT?

Dolly and her aunt Dorothy Jo have cowritten songs, starting when Dolly was a teenager!

When Dolly was first trying to break into the music industry, her uncle Bill helped her hit the ground running by introducing her to music industry folks and getting her performance gigs.

Dolly says she learned all about working hard from her dad, who worked day and night to provide for their family. She credits her strong work ethic to him!

Who are the people in your life you can turn to for help achieving your dreams?

List them here:

_____

_____

_____

_____

_____

_____

_____

_____

_____

_____

_____

_____

_____

_____

_____

_____

_____

Need a Dolly-style pep talk to inspire you to chase your dreams and work hard at them? Look no further!

Do you know the story *The Little Engine That Could*? That was one of the first books Dolly remembers reading, and now she thinks of herself as the little engine that could . . . and *did*. And you can, too!

Dream big but, like Dolly, be a doer, not *just* a dreamer. As Dolly says, **"Do not confuse dreams with wishes."** You've gotta do more than just wish upon a star for your dreams to come true!

Cherish the folks who support you and your dreams (like Dolly's uncle Bill did for her) and don't pay any mind to the people who don't!

Be patient with yourself and your progress. The road to success is long and winding, but you will get there if you never give up!

Pay It Forward

"I love being able to do things that create opportunities for others . . ."

Helping folks in need is important no matter who you are or where you come from. Giving back is especially important to Dolly, and she pays her success forward by using her money *and* time *and* talent to help others!

And Dolly knows firsthand how helpful the kindness of strangers can be. When she was a teenager, her uncle Bill took her to the Grand Ole Opry—a *super* famous country music venue in Nashville—to try to get her onstage to perform. Another performer, Jimmy C. Newman, kindly let Dolly take his place, and she got to fulfill her dream of performing at the Grand Ole Opry for the first time at a really young age.

Would Dolly be the star she is today without the help of Jimmy C. Newman (and many others along the way)? Did Jimmy know that that act of kindness would help launch one of country music's most famous stars?

HOW HAS DOLLY HELPED OTHERS?

Here are just a *few* of the things Dolly has done to pay it forward through the years:

She founded the Imagination Library, which mails one million free books every month to kids in preschool to help them learn to read!

She donated money to Vanderbilt University to help with their development of the Moderna vaccine during the COVID-19 pandemic, which eventually saved thousands of lives.

She invested profits from Whitney Houston's version of "I Will Always Love You" in an office complex in a historically Black neighborhood in Nashville, Tennessee.

She partners and performs with young, up-and-coming musicians, like her goddaughter Miley Cyrus and Kelsea Ballerini, lending her star power to the generations coming up behind her.

She founded her Dollywood theme park in the Great Smoky Mountains region of Tennessee, which provides jobs and brings business and income to the community that brought her up.

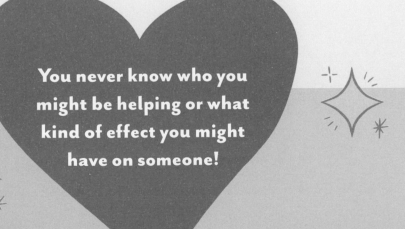

You never know who you might be helping or what kind of effect you might have on someone!

*"I'll go to my grave doin' everything
I can to make the world
a better place and myself
a better person."*

There are so many ways Dolly has helped others, and there are so many ways *you* can help others, too, even if you aren't opening your own theme park or donating millions of books to kids every year (yet!). Welcoming others into your life and heart, especially when they seem like they could use a smile from a stranger, is a great way to build bridges.

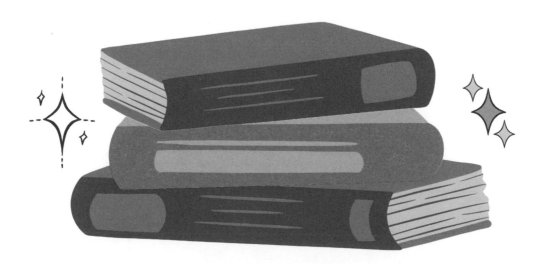

What's one way you've paid it forward to help someone you don't really know? Even if you can't think of a past example, think of potential ways you *could* help others in the future, like:

donating clothes you've outgrown

putting on a bake sale and giving the money you make to a charity

inviting a new kid at school to sit at your lunch table

WRITE YOUR IDEAS HERE!

Paying it forward doesn't always have to be about helping strangers. You can also help out the people you know: your friends and family. They'd do the same for you if you needed a hand, and you helping out someone you know just might inspire *them* to help *another person* out down the road. That's how you can help create a whole community of kindness and generosity that's so much bigger than just you.

What are some ways you could help out your friends or family right now? Brainstorm some ideas on the facing page and then put them into action!

Here are a few suggestions to get you going:

Offer to help a neighbor carry their groceries or walk their dog.

Use your allowance to buy a friend a snack at lunchtime.

Offer to help a classmate study for a test.

BRAINSTORM WAYS TO HELP

We can all get a little caught up in our own lives sometimes! If you need some inspiration to remember to pay it forward, well, here ya go.

Aren't sure where to start paying it forward? As Dolly says, **"Never ignore your roots, your home, or your hair!"**

As Dolly would say: **"Leave something good in every day."**

You may never even know all the effects lending a helping hand might have—but that's okay. Just trust good deeds lead to more good deeds that **"create a legacy that inspires others to dream more, learn more, do more, and become more."**

Keep
Creativity
Flowing

"If I had to choose just one thing to be, I would choose to be a songwriter."

One thing Dolly Parton is for sure is *creative*! It seems like she's *always* creating—songs, stories, fun outfits—and guess what? You can be just as creative as Dolly.

Inspiration for your creativity can come from anywhere and everywhere. The first song Dolly ever wrote, when she was five or six years old, was about a doll her mama made for her. (The song was called "Little Tiny Tassletop.") Dolly sang about the doll and the feelings she had about the doll, and her mama wrote the song down and saved it in an old shoebox for years.

Dolly POP QUIZ

What other (seemingly random) things has Dolly written songs about?

a) An old coat

b) The state of Texas

c) Her father's work boots

d) The morning breeze

e) All of the above!

Answer: e) All of the above!

Being creative can really help you express yourself and your feelings. All those feels need to have someplace to go, right? One of Dolly's main creative outlets is songwriting (duh, you knew that already!). She often writes songs to help her work through whatever's going on in her life.

DOLLY'S MOVIE SOUNDTRACKS:

Dolly has also written songs for some of the movies she's been in, like:

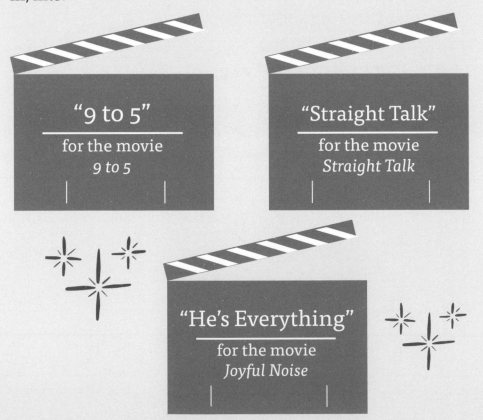

"9 to 5"
for the movie
9 to 5

"Straight Talk"
for the movie
Straight Talk

"He's Everything"
for the movie
Joyful Noise

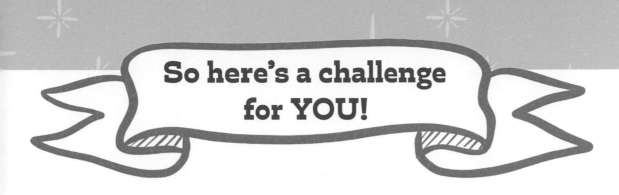

So here's a challenge for YOU!

Look around wherever you are and pick one thing you can see—a tree, a school bus, your brother's smelly ol' shoe, anything. Flip to page 132 and write a song about that thing on the blank songwriting pages.

The more creative and imaginative and out there, the better!

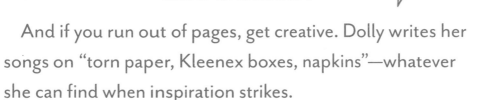

And if you run out of pages, get creative. Dolly writes her songs on "torn paper, Kleenex boxes, napkins"—whatever she can find when inspiration strikes.

You can also find inspiration by trying out new things. Dolly's first creative love may be songwriting, but she channels her creativity in so many directions.

HOW HAS DOLLY EXPRESSED HERSELF CREATIVELY?

★ written books—on her own and with different collaborators, such as James Patterson

★ developed and produced shows for Netflix

★ written and performed country music, pop music, spiritual music, songs for a Broadway musical, and even collaborated on an EDM (electronic dance music) song

★ acted in movies

★ opened a theme park

★ influenced and inspired younger musicians and actors, such as her goddaughter Miley Cyrus and Lil Nas X, who covered her song "Jolene"

Golly, that Dolly is always finding new ways to express herself! What are some new creative outlets you want to try?

List them here:

_____

_____

_____

_____

_____

_____

_____

_____

_____

_____

_____

_____

_____

You may think you know the *one* thing you're good at, but you'll never know what *else* you could be GREAT at unless you try something new.

DOLLY PEP TALK!

Next time you're feeling stuck creatively, remember all the different ways Dolly has found to express herself creatively, and think about these gems for inspiration:

It's never too late to try something new and get creative with it—as Dolly says, **"Getting old don't mean you can't be creative."**

Inspiration can hit **"anywhere, anytime, anyplace,"** Dolly says—so **"try to be open to it and always try to be ready"** by keeping a notebook or recorder around to capture ideas when they come.

You don't need to be able to paint or draw or sculpt to make something beautiful! Dolly aims to **"paint a picture"** with the words in her songs.

Dolly says, **"I'm not going to limit myself just because people won't accept the fact that I can do something else."**

Channel your inner Dolly! Don't let anyone stifle your creativity.

When You're Feeling Overwhelmed

"I'm always
the one who's
up, the one who
carries the ball."

Have you ever felt like you have *so* much going on—schoolwork, chores, family time, friend time, extracurricular activities—that you feel just *totally* overwhelmed?

We all get overwhelmed sometimes, and, yes, that includes Dolly Parton herself. Dolly has worked herself so hard that she's ended up feeling sick and tired, even losing her voice and needing medical treatment. You can learn from Dolly's mistakes as well as her achievements: you never want to let yourself get so overwhelmed or over-worked that you start to feel sick.

It's important to take care of yourself, and that means taking breaks, making time for fun and calming activities, and maybe even taking catnaps (like Dolly does) during long days.

Those big dreams of yours should motivate you to work hard, but it's totally okay to take a break when you need to. Your dreams'll still be there when you get back to them!

STOP what you're doing and take a break **RIGHT NOW.**

One way to take a break and bring some calm to your day when you're feeling overwhelmed is by taking deep breaths and exhaling slowly. Dolly meditates early in the morning when she wakes up. Try it!

Breathe in . . . breathe out.

Breathe in . . . breathe out.

Breathe in . . . breathe out.

Breathe in . . . breathe out.

Breathe in . . . breathe out.

Do you feel calmer now?
Hope so!

Now build on that calm feeling by making a playlist of relaxing tunes. Whenever you feel stressed, you can press pause on whatever you're doing and press play on this playlist!

Here's the perfect soothing first track to get you started:

"Islands in the Stream" by Dolly Parton and Kenny Rogers

_____

_____

_____

_____

_____

_____

_____

_____

_____

_____

_____

_____

_____

_____

"I think if you stay true to your roots, and home is always in your heart and in your head, you'll succeed."

Hopefully, your home is one place where you can really kick back and relax—like Dolly's home is for her. Dolly uses her time at home in Tennessee to recharge. She spends time with family members and loved ones, cooks, goes on walks and picnics, and—of course—reads a lot. What she doesn't do at home is work too hard!

HOME IS WHERE THE HEART IS

What makes Dolly's home so relaxing?

It's on a small road set back from the main road, so it's quiet.

There's a front porch where she and her husband, Carl, can sit outside and enjoy privacy.

There's a dedicated space for Dolly to meditate and pray, which is very important to her.

Where is one place you feel calm and relaxed (home or not)? Draw it here so you can always revisit it, even if you can't get there IRL:

Take one more *deeeeeep* breath in and out. And remember:

In addition to taking time to relax, also take time to do things you love that *aren't* work—or as Dolly puts it, **"Don't get so busy making a living that you forget to make a life."**

Be strict about taking breaks—for example, Dolly says she **"depends a lot on prayer and meditation"**—and it will become part of your routine.

Doing breathing exercises to calm down doesn't have to happen in a special meditation room or even indoors. You can do what Dolly does: **"Go out and smell the air after a good, hard rain."**

Setbacks
and
New Starts

"Sometimes a failure is just a success dressed in different clothes."

Listen up: we *all* fail or face bumps in the road sometimes. Seriously, everyone!

It may seem like Dolly's life is perfect, and her path to success and stardom has been easy—but nope. Dolly has dealt with hardships, setbacks, and full-on failures along the way, and they'll keep on coming. 'Cause that's life.

How does Dolly deal? And how can *you* deal when you're facing a failure or something doesn't go as planned?

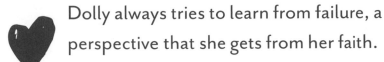 Dolly always tries to learn from failure, a perspective that she gets from her faith.

When something is harder than expected, there are lots of ways to work with it—including being open to changing your plan and coming up with a new approach that could be even better!

You can also lean on a friend or family member for a helping hand.

For example, when Dolly was a kid, she loved music and performing, but she couldn't read or write music—so her best friend, Judy, wrote down all her music for her as Dolly would come up with lyrics and tunes. Judy and Dolly are *still* BFFs (that last *F* means forever, duh), and Judy is *still* involved in Dolly's career. Dolly overcame that hurdle the way she does all the time. She asked for help— and her pal Judy was happy to be there for her.

QUIZ

How Dolly are you in your handling of setbacks or failures? Take this quiz to find out!

1. The night before a big project is due, the computer crashes and all your work disappears. How do you react?

a) Panic. Cry. Scream. Repeat.

b) Ask an adult to write a note to your teacher explaining what happened and asking for a deadline extension.

c) Start the project all over again, and this time, you save the work as you go.

2. You didn't get the lead in the school play. So you . . .

a) Trash talk the person who was cast instead.

b) Ask the theater teacher for extra coaching during free periods.

c) Join the crew to learn all you can about the theater process—you might just find out you love backstage work as much as being onstage!

3. Your totally _brilliant_ idea for a school fundraiser didn't win the student council vote—someone else's did. What's your next step?

    a) Storm out of the meeting before it's over so you can cry in the bathroom.

    b) Ask someone to team up and brainstorm for the next one.

    c) Reread your proposal and think about how you can improve it next time.

If you answered . . .

Mostly As: It's A-okay to lean into your emotional response when a setback pops up—Dolly is all about feeling feelings as they come! But after you've worked through all the feels, you might try taking some positive action, either by asking someone for help or seeing what you can learn from the setback (or both!).

Mostly Bs: You know how important and calming asking for help can be—just like Dolly does! Make sure you know who you can count on in your life to help out when you need it (and vice versa— friendship and helping out goes both ways).

Mostly Cs: You're _so_ Dolly, always looking to learn something, even and especially when things get really hard or you face a failure. Dolly would be proud!

"I'm not afraid to try anything, and I'm certainly not afraid to fail."

Setbacks can come from the outside (like someone tearing you down) or the inside (like self-doubt). Don't let setbacks limit your dreams!

Dolly had to carve out her own space and role in the country music scene and the bigger entertainment industry because there was no one quite like her in music or the movies.

She turned that challenge into an advantage and embraced being different. Being different made her a trailblazer. If other people didn't want to accept that she could do anything, well, tough! Dolly found a way to do it her way, often with the support of her lifetime friends and family like Judy and her husband, Carl.

Setbacks can come from inside, too, from self-doubt or confidence issues. Dolly may seem like she's always cool as a cucumber, but she's had self-esteem issues, too.

For instance, before she gave a commencement speech at the University of Tennessee, she was plagued with doubt: Why would these graduates want to hear anything li'l ol' Dolly had to say? She took a bunch of deep breaths, gave herself a pep talk backstage, and when she walked out onstage, the warm welcome she got from the university faculty and students gave her the extra boost of confidence she needed. She was able to find the strength to just *be herself* with the students that day.

PEP TALK!

This time, *give yourself* a pep talk! Imagine it in Dolly's voice, if that helps— she believes in you.

Draft that pep talk here:

_____

_____

_____

_____

_____

_____

_____

_____

_____

_____

_____

_____

_____

_____

When You're Feeling Blue

"I put all my feelings, my very soul, into my writing."

When Dolly was a kid, her family was down on their luck. One winter, Dolly needed a coat, but her family couldn't afford a new one—so her mama sewed her one made out of a patchwork of scraps of fabric. Dolly loved the coat and was excited to wear it to school, but when she did, her classmates all laughed at her coat made of "rags." Their teasing made Dolly feel bad, like she wasn't good enough.

Years later, Dolly turned that painful memory into "Coat of Many Colors," a smash hit.

Dolly often writes songs about what she's feeling, even if she never shares the songs with the public. Writing about her experiences, even a long time later, helps her find strength. And she's found that it helps other people who might be feeling the same way when they listen to them!

Which of these things is true about "Coat of Many Colors"?

a) Dolly originally wrote the song on the back of a dry-cleaning receipt.

b) Dolly calls the song "a world of things" because it talks about bullying, acceptance, love, and more.

c) Dolly is proud of how many people love "Coat of Many Colors" and how it has a healing effect on some people who are struggling in one way or another.

d) All of the above!

QUIZ

Life can knock you down, but how do you handle it when it does? Take this quiz to find out how Dolly-like your response is!

1. When someone teases you at school, you . . .

   a) Tease them right back—it's only fair!

   b) Tell an adult what's going on.

   c) Channel your hurt feelings into a creative outlet.

2. When you feel sad, you . . .

   a) Ignore the feelings and go on with your day like everything is fine.

   b) Talk to a friend or family member about it.

   c) Take the time to feel your feelings because a heart needs time to heal (as Dolly says in her song "I'm in No Condition").

3. You show up to a school dance and you're dressed very differently from everyone else, making you stand out. What do you do?

a) Leave the dance before someone makes fun of how you're dressed.

b) Find a friendly face and stick by their side the whole night.

c) Hold your head up high and try to have fun anyway!

If you answered . . .

Mostly As: You often go on the defensive and push your feelings away, but Dolly says that it's important to feel all your feelings, good and bad, happy and sad. That's what makes us human!

Mostly Bs: You're very open with your feelings and often rely on trusted loved ones to help you through, just like Dolly does with her family and close friends. A good support network is important.

Mostly Cs: Are you sure your name isn't Dolly Parton? Well, Dolly would be proud of how you handled yourself—allowing yourself to feel the hurt but also trying to persevere.

"You have to work hard at being happy, just like you have to work hard at being miserable."

Life has not always been easy on Dolly—but she climbs every mountain that appears in front of her. In fact, Dolly grew up surrounded by the Appalachian Mountains, and the music of that region had a major impact on her life.

The music Dolly grew up around has inspired her songwriting, but one of the things that makes Dolly so special is that she sets her songs to a tempo all her own and finds a way to move forward, even when a little mud gets on her bedazzled boots.

So, listen up!

No matter who is trying to bring you down, or whatever problems you're facing, remember how Dolly always honors her feelings and then walks on, head held high, prouder than proud.

WHAT IS APPALACHIAN MUSIC?

 Appalachian music is folk music that blends Anglo-Saxon ballads, a German dulcimer, and African American banjo and string band sounds.

 The music style is unique because of its melancholy, moody sound.

 Many Appalachian songs are about suffering and the hardships of life.

Dolly PEP TALK!

The next time you're feeling blue, try . . .

Going for a walk or playing a game outside. Fresh air is important! When Dolly was growing up, she and her siblings played outdoors all the time.

Talking to a loved one about those blues you're feeling. You can work together to find a solution, or not—sometimes it just helps to be heard.

Reading a book! Dolly loves to read and always has. It can be relaxing and distracting to get lost in a good story.

Channeling your blue feelings into something creative, be it writing a song or painting a picture or crafting a story. As Dolly says about herself, **"Whatever it is, I can say it in a song, in my own way."**

Exercising. Sometimes getting up and being active—even when you really don't feel like it—can help improve your mood.

And speaking of channeling your blues into creativity, why not try writing a song? Use the lyrics of "Coat of Many Colors" as inspiration—pay attention to how Dolly tells her story through the music. How does she set the scene? How does she describe what happened and the feelings it brought up?

Feeling Angry

"People will use
you as long as
you let them."

Raise your hand if you've ever felt angry!

Oh, look, every person on earth (and probably even some aliens in outer space) has a hand raised—including Dolly.

That's 'cause *everyone* feels angry sometimes. Feeling angry is totally okay and normal. The question is, how do you deal with that anger so you don't feel angry *all the time*?

You can go right to the source of the anger, like Dolly did when she turned forty. She wrote letters and made phone calls to confront some family members and business associates who had been taking advantage of her through the years. Telling those folks they had no control over her allowed Dolly to "get all the grief and worries over irresponsible people" outta her life. She could move forward without angry feelings holding her back. ***And you can, too!***

Music can be a great way to channel angry feelings—and so can physical activity. So why not combine those two and have an **ANGRY DANCE PARTY?!**

What songs would you put on your **ANGRY DANCE PARTY** playlist? Are they fast, slow, emotional, totally wordless? Are there any Dolly Parton songs on there? (Psst. Check out "Dumb Blonde" or "I Wasted My Tears.")

And what kind of dance moves will you be showing off at this dance session? The more energetic, the better!

Okay, you ready?

DANCE THAT ANGER OUT!

"I've often said I don't lose my temper as much as I use it."

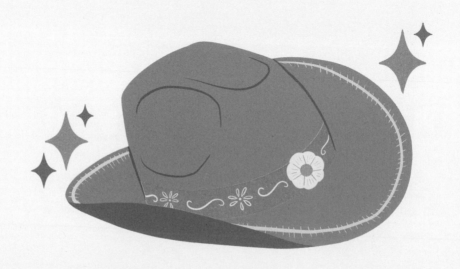

Another way to cope with angry feelings is to *use* them. You can channel your anger into something productive, like taking action against an injustice. Let your anger motivate you to make a change, big or small.

That could mean making a change in your own life that will keep you striving to be the best *you* you can be, like Dolly did when she fired a musician in her band after he criticized her show costumes. (As she pointed out on tour, the drum machine she replaced him with saved her money and didn't talk back!) Or it could mean getting involved in activism for an issue or a cause you care about.

How you use your anger is up to you, but it's important to make sure you don't just let it simmer and boil inside of you. Use it for good. You'll be happy you did.

Dolly PEP TALK!

The next time you feel angry, try:

Taking some time for yourself to deal with your anger, like Dolly and her husband, Carl, do whenever they have a tiff.

Confronting the source of your anger so you can move forward.

Using your anger to make change and fight injustice, big or small.

Channeling that anger into an activity that will burn some angry energy and emotions—like a dance party or writing in a journal. Dolly says that writing music is her form of therapy!

Always remember: It's totally okay to feel angry. It's just a part of life!

Being a True-Blue Friend (and Ex-Friend)

"If you see someone without a smile today, give 'em yours."

A true-blue friend, as Dolly knows, is someone who really knows and loves you. You support each other and trust each other, whether you've known each other for ten years or ten minutes.

What are the most important ingredients
when it comes to a friendship?

According to Dolly:

Dolly says she will always be honest and expects honesty in return from her friends, family, and people she works with.

Trust is key in any relationship, and it builds over time. Dolly says you can build trust by being true to your word, all the time, even for small things. It builds trust for the big stuff.

Building that trust eventually leads to respect. People know you're reliable and they'll be there for you because they know you'll be there for them.

All of the above shows how much you love and care for someone!

"I've always said I will step over you or around you to get where I'm going, but I will never step on you."

Dolly has a huge heart, and that means she's always welcoming people into her life, either by giving back to her community (or beyond her community, to people she doesn't even know), lending a helping hand to someone who needs it, or just by striving to be a good friend.

Time to dig deep into those personal relationships!
How can you be a good friend
like Dolly? What matters most in a friendship?
These are important questions to keep in mind.

**Jot down some of
your answers here:**

_____

_____

_____

_____

_____

_____

_____

_____

_____

_____

_____

_____

_____

_____

_____

_____

One way you can express your love and admiration for a friend is to write them a song that talks about all the things you love about them! Why not give it a try?

Use the space on the facing page to write a Dolly-like song to your bestie.

PS: It doesn't have to rhyme if you don't want it to!

WRITE YOUR SONG

_____

_____

_____

_____

_____

_____

_____

_____

_____

_____

_____

_____

_____

_____

_____

_____

_____

_____

_____

Have you ever had a fight with a friend? Even *true-blue* friends fight sometimes.

In the 1970s, Dolly was working with fellow country music star Porter Wagoner on *The Porter Wagoner Show*. Being on the show was a big break for Dolly, but also *a lot* of work. She and Porter didn't always get along. (In fact, they started fighting like cats and dogs just six months into their long partnership!) After a while, Dolly knew she wanted to move on to try new things—like different music styles and acting in movies. So it was time for Dolly to make like a banana and split from *The Porter Wagoner Show*.

Porter wasn't too happy Dolly wanted to leave his show but despite all the fighting, Dolly knew she was "going to go, one way or another."

So Dolly did what she always does; what she's best at—she put all that tension and emotion into a song. And she left Porter's show and ended their friendship.

It takes strength to say good-bye, but sometimes it's the right thing to do. You deserve to have good friends around you who love and care for you as much as you love and care for them. It's the Dolly Parton way.

I WILL ALWAYS LOVE YOU

- The song Dolly wrote about parting ways with Porter is called "I Will Always Love You."

- Dolly took the high road—dedicating this song to Porter as she left the show and ended their friendship. It resulted in her writing one of her most famous songs!

- The song became a No. 1 hit for Dolly.

- Elvis Presley wanted to record it, and Whitney Houston recorded it in the early nineties, taking "I Will Always Love You" to worldwide fame.

QUIZ

Can you tell when a friendship is worth holding on to or when you might need to take a break from each other, like Dolly did with Porter? Take this quiz to find out!

1. When you need help with something, your friend . . .

    a) Totally ghosts you

    b) Lends a hand without you even asking

    c) Helps if you promise them a favor in return

2. If you and your friend were paired up for a school project, you'd feel . . .

    a) Dread. You *know* you're going to end up doing *all* the work.

    b) Sooooo excited! You always have your best ideas when you two are working together!

    c) Relieved. It's always better to be paired up with a friendly face, and you can split the workload fifty-fifty.

3. If you make plans with this friend, you know . . .

a) There's a 75 percent chance they'll bail.

b) Whatever you've got planned is going to be *the most* fun ever.

c) You don't usually hang out with this friend one-on-one, but you always have fun together in a group.

If you answered . . .

Mostly As: Sounds like this friend isn't much of a friend at all—maybe it's time to take a friendship break!

Mostly Bs: This is a true-blue, lifelong friend (like Dolly and her best friend from childhood, Judy) and you should keep them around.

Mostly Cs: This friend is more like an acquaintance, but you can definitely get closer! It's important to be open and honest with your friends to make sure you're on the same page about what you both expect out of a friendship—simple as that.

"I write what I write, say what I say, 'cause I feel what I feel."

Dolly POP QUIZ

Which of these friendship experiences has Dolly dealt with?

a) Finding out a family member was telling stories about her to the tabloids

b) Having people try to blackmail her

c) Ending a long professional and personal partnership with grace

d) Working with close friends to the tune of lots of success

e) All of the above!

Answer: e) All of the above!

The rift between Dolly and Porter lasted for many years. But after a good long while, they eventually made up and sang "I Will Always Love You" onstage together during an episode of her television variety show, *Dolly*. Dolly was also by Porter's side at the end of his life.

We can all learn a little something from Dolly's forgiveness of her old partner, Porter. You don't have to forgive everyone who's ever wronged you, but compassion is important to Dolly, and her big ol' heart has a lot of room for forgiveness in it. And as important as it is to forgive others, it's just as important to be able to apologize and ask for forgiveness when you know *you're* in the wrong.

Do you have room in your heart to forgive? Fill in the heart image below with alllllll the things you have room for!

Is there someone in your life who's asking for your forgiveness? Could be a friend who let you down when you needed 'em, a sibling who got you in trouble with your parents, or someone who hurt your feelings someway or somehow.

It's okay if you're not ready to forgive yet. But if and when you are, why not try writing a letter first before having the real-life forgiveness conversation with that person? If a letter doesn't feel right, try putting your thoughts into a song. As Dolly says, "Everybody can understand a song."

You don't have to deliver the letter or perform the song, but it might help to get all your thoughts and feelings out. Imagine you're talking directly to them and addressing what they did to upset you and why you want to forgive them.

I'm sorry.

WRITE A LETTER

_____
_____
_____
_____
_____
_____
_____
_____
_____
_____
_____
_____
_____
_____
_____
_____
_____
_____
_____

"As soon as you realize something is a problem, you should fix it. . . . I would never dream of hurting somebody on purpose."

Offering someone your forgiveness doesn't have to mean welcoming that person back into your life, like Dolly did with Porter. But hopefully forgiving someone will make you feel more at peace 'cause you're no longer holding a grudge or feeling upset.

And remember, sometimes you might be on the apologizing end of the forgiveness equation! You would probably never hurt someone's feelings on purpose, right? Even so, it's pretty darn likely that you might need to ask someone for forgiveness one day.

When that happens, wear your compassion hat
(or compassion wig, to be more Dolly-like), and:

LISTEN

Listen when that person
explains why they're upset.

THINK

Think long and hard about what
you did and why it hurt.

APOLOGIZE

Apologize in a heartfelt
and genuine way.

Dolly PEP TALK!

Even the best friendships can have lots of ups and downs. Sometimes good friends fight, and sometimes fighting can even be a good thing. It can help you understand things about your friend that you might not have before. In Dolly's own words:

"You always need a good friend to lift you up, tell you the truth, and if you're lucky, sing a song with!"

"In all relationships—no matter what they are—you have to respect each other."

To Speak Up, Stand Up

"I love peace and harmony, but when you step in my territory, I will call you on it."

Have you ever found yourself in a situation where you need to stand up for yourself or for someone else?

Well, so has Dolly!

Dolly Parton always tries to be honest and candid (and she expects the same in return from her friends and family!). That means Dolly's true to herself and also not afraid to speak up and say what's on her mind. Inspiring, right?

Speaking your truth can sometimes feel awkward or uncomfortable, and you may worry that people won't like or accept you. That's a totally reasonable feeling! But channel your inner Dolly and remember that speaking your truth and standing up for what you believe in is important and can make you a better friend and a better person.

WAYS DOLLY SPEAKS HER TRUTH:

Saying no when Elvis Presley wanted to record "I Will Always Love You" because he wanted to buy the full rights.

No, Elvis.

Focusing her charitable efforts where her heart and values lie, especially working to help people in the Appalachian region.

Pushing back on Porter Wagoner's mean jokes on-air.

Expressing her belief in equality over and over—including gay folks' right to marriage, the assertion that Black lives matter just as much as any other life, and women's equality as a "feminist in practice" as she says she has always been.

QUIZ

How likely are *you* to speak *your* truth? Take this quiz to find out!

1. Your best friend shows you her first-day-of-school outfit and wants you to match, but you hate it. You say:

    a)   "Not my style, but let's twin another time!"

    b)   "I wouldn't be caught dead in that and you shouldn't, either!"

    c)   You agree to match and spend the days leading up to school with a pit in your stomach.

2. You witness someone getting bullied at school. You:

    a)   Get the nearest adult to intervene, fast.

    b)   Step in and stand up for the bullied with a quick one-liner, and then take the victim aside to comfort them.

    c)   Walk away pretending you didn't see or hear anything.

3. There's a big protest this weekend for a cause that's close to your heart. You:

a) Ask your parents if they'll go with you because you're passionate about the cause.

b) Help organize the protest!

c) Stay home because even though you want to join in, you're afraid what other people will say about you if you do.

If you answered . . .

Mostly As: You're not afraid to speak up for what you believe in, and in a way that often gets people to listen. Just like Dolly!

Mostly Bs: You're all action! You might want to soften the message sometimes, but in general, great job speaking your truth.

Mostly Cs: You have strong beliefs, but you need a little more practice speaking up. Don't worry. It's not easy to take a stand. Just be ready for the next chance you get.

"I'm open and I'm honest."

Dolly doesn't just speak her truth in interviews and in her private life—she does it in her songs, too! Ever since she got started in the music biz, Dolly has been using her songs to tell stories—about the people of Appalachia (especially the women she grew up around), about her faith, and about the way she sees the world.

Speaking your truth, mind, and values can take different forms—public protest, artistic expression, and even private conversations—and each one can make an impact. Choose which way works best for you and don't be afraid to be honest about your opinions. (But also remember that there's no need to hurt someone's feelings in the name of honesty! Dolly never said it was easy. . . .)

For Dolly, the easiest way to express herself is in song. Try to channel your inner Dolly and use the pages at the back of the book to write a song that tells your truth. It can be funny, serious, or heartfelt—whatever's in your heart is what Dolly would want you to sing about.

There's no better Dolly advice about speaking out and standing up than this nugget of truth:

I don't dillydally. If there's something going on, I just say it.

Shine Bright

"You don't have to look like everybody else. You don't have to be a raving beauty to be special and to be beautiful."

First things first: you can shine bright *however* you choose to . . . just like Dolly does!

Dolly's mama and her church disapproved of Dolly wearing makeup, and the other girls at her school thought Dolly looked "trashy" with her super-teased blond hairdo. But that style eventually became Dolly's signature look. She wanted her outside to match her bright, bold, and colorful inside.

As Dolly got older and was getting more famous, she continued to fight against judgments people would make about her, especially about her so-called "hillbilly" or "trailer trash" roots. She's proud of where she came from, and everything that comes along with it, including her accent. It's all part of what makes Dolly . . . *Dolly.*

Other people might try to define or dismiss you

because of how you look, sound, act, or anything else, but don't let 'em. You know yourself, and you can shine bright like a rhinestone even when other people try to dull your sparkle!

Fill out the gem on the next page with all the things that make you shine bright from the inside out—list one on each facet.

Here are some ideas to get you thinking:

I can make people laugh.

I love helping people.

I am a good listener.

I am a great problem solver.

I am very creative.

Turn back to this page whenever you need a reminder of all the inner ways you shine!

"Being a star just means that you find your own special place and you shine where you are."

Dolly made her outside match her sparkly inside. Now that *you've* thought about the gem that *you* are, how can you show that bright, shiny inside to the outside world? How can you express your inner rhinestone?

How will you craft a signature personal style like Dolly did? How will you express your inner shine? Write your thoughts below.

_____

_____

_____

_____

_____

_____

_____

_____

DOLLY POP QUIZ

What did Dolly use as natural makeup when she was young and couldn't afford the store-bought stuff?

a)   Red berries as lipstick

b)   Burnt matches as eyeliner

c)   Honeysuckle as perfume

d)   All of the above!

Answer: d) All of the above!

Dolly PEP TALK!

Feel free to channel Dolly's confident shine whenever you need a little boost:

"You need to really believe in what you've got to offer, what your talent is—and if you believe, that gives you strength."

"I look totally artificial, but I am totally real, as a writer, as a professional, as a human being."

"A peacock that rests on its feathers is just another turkey." In other words, show your beautiful feathers off, loud and proud!

Define Your Faith

"You have to believe."

Faiths and beliefs come in all shapes and sizes. Dolly's faith is based in Christianity, but her beliefs are also all her own. She grew up going to church—she loved all the singing, of course—and being Christian is a big part of what made her who she is.

But Dolly's faith isn't just about church, and your own faith doesn't have to just be tied to religion, either. Dolly says that in her experience being poor and living in the back country that "you have to believe," meaning all she had was her faith to lean on to trust that things would work out.

Dolly's the first to admit that she's no saint. But her faith and spirituality and prayers carry her through as she tries to be the best Dolly she can be.

What contributes to your faith, beliefs, and values? (Being kind? Taking care of others? Being humble?) What do you believe in? How does *your* faith push you to be the best *you* that you can be?

Jot down your thoughts here:

_____

_____

_____

_____

_____

_____

_____

_____

_____

_____

_____

_____

_____

_____

_____

You already know that Dolly often pours her feelings and thoughts about her life into her songwriting, but did you know that includes her faith? For example, in 2019, she collaborated on a song with Galantis called "Faith." She also wrote a song about her faith called "He's Everything" for her 2012 movie with Queen Latifah called *Joyful Noise.*

Use the space on the facing page to jot down some thoughts or lyrics about your own faith, however you feel and express it.

Write your thoughts here:

_____
_____
_____
_____
_____
_____
_____
_____
_____
_____
_____
_____
_____
_____
_____
_____
_____
_____
_____
_____
_____

"I always count my blessings far more than I count my money."

Dolly is a Christian, but a lot of her ideas about faith don't just apply to Christianity specifically. Here are some of Dolly's core beliefs that may help you along the way:

Dolly believes in "God clues," little signs that often point her in the right direction, especially when she's unsure of what path to take.

Try to care, rather than judge.

When you're faced with a failure, look for the lesson in the failure, rather than wallowing in it.

Dolly gets the same feeling from praying that some people get from exercising— she feels more alert after and extra excited about the day to come.

If someone is causing trouble or problems in your life, try to think about how you can grow and learn by dealing with them compassionately.

Everybody has their own journey. They have their own way of doing things. And who am I to judge?

I think everybody should be allowed to be who they are, and to love who they love.

There are so many great, glorious pieces of good in the world.

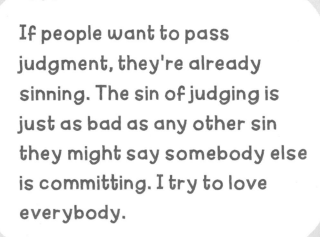

If people want to pass judgment, they're already sinning. The sin of judging is just as bad as any other sin they might say somebody else is committing. I try to love everybody.

108

Be Yourself

"Everybody should look and be whatever makes them comfortable so their inner self . . . can shine."

When Dolly was about nine years old, she had to go to a new school because her old one burned down. The kids at the new school were wealthier than the kids at her old one, and they made fun of Dolly for being poor. (*Rude!*) When the teacher once asked the class what they'd had for breakfast, Dolly was embarrassed that she'd had biscuits and gravy, knowing her classmates would make fun of it, so she told a tall tale about the great, big, delicious breakfast she'd had that day.

As Dolly's grown up, though, she's become more and more comfortable with who she is and where she came from. Nowadays, Dolly dresses how she likes, writes and records the kinds of music she loves, manages her business how she sees fit, and speaks her mind honestly.

Dolly's true and authentic to herself. And you can be, too!

What are the things that make you YOU?

Using the two frames here, draw yourself as you see you— and don't forget to set yourself in the places where you feel happiest!

"I'd rather be an honest person than a good liar."

Has Dolly dealt with self-doubt and self-esteem issues? Of course she has. She's struggled with feeling comfortable in and loving her body, standing up for herself, living with failures and setbacks and betrayals, and all the invasive questions about her personal life that come with being famous. For example, about how she and her husband, Carl, spend lots of time apart. Some people think that's odd and try to tear Dolly down because of it. But Dolly and Carl do what works for them! As she says, "We enjoy the stuff we enjoy" and "get along great." Everyone struggles with confidence issues sometimes. But take it from Dolly: being true to yourself and leaning into your confidence is the best remedy for self-doubt.

Here are a few key questions to ask yourself to make sure you're always being true to who you are in any situation:

✱ How does this feel in my gut?

✱ Will I feel proud of this choice or how I acted when I look back on it later?

✱ Am I doing this because I want to or because someone else wants me to?

✱ Do I feel like my truest, best self right now?

✱ If I saw someone else doing this, how would I feel? Envious, upset, amused, or proud?

No matter who you are, the best advice is to just be YOU! Here's some more inspiration from Dolly to celebrate the _you_ that you are:

"I never felt I belonged. Never belonged in my whole life, even as a little kid. I was just different and so I never really found my place till I moved to Nashville and got in the music business. That was my real place, so I fit in."

"I'm proud of my hillbilly, white-trash background. If that's who you are, that's who you are. It'll show up once in a while."

"I've had to go against all kinds of people through the years just to be myself."

"I'm very real where it counts, and that's inside."

Having Fun

"There is nothin' I like better than goin' home to have a few weeks off."

When Dolly was young, she had to use her imagination and creativity to have fun. Her family didn't have a TV, or much else for that matter, but they made their own entertainment.

Here are some ways the Partons made their own fun:

 Dolly's always loved reading! The walls of her house were covered in newspaper, so she'd read the walls if there wasn't a book around.

 Dolly grew up hearing her family tell and retell Bible stories.

 Dolly used to pretend that the Partons' front porch was a stage and a tin can on a stick was a microphone. She'd sing songs she made up and pretend some chickens were her audience.

HAVE FUN LIKE DOLLY

- Use your imagination to play pretend and act out something cool and exciting like Dolly did when she pretended her porch was a stage.

- Throw a dance party—with your friends, your favorite stuffed animals, or just yourself!

- Connect with nature—take a long walk, play a game outside, or go fishing (one of Dolly's favorite pastimes).

- Cook or bake something new and delicious!

- Watch your favorite Dolly Parton movie. Don't forget the popcorn!

- Do a karaoke night featuring your favorite Dolly Parton songs.

- Hit up a wig store with a friend and see who can find the funkiest (or most Dolly-like) wig first.

- Go to a vintage clothing store and search for the most rhinestone-bedazzled Dolly Parton outfit you can find!

Dolly's life proves that you can have fun anywhere, anytime—all it takes is a little imagination and the right attitude. That imagination fueled her career and built up her love of music and performance.

QUIZ

How Dolly-like are you when it comes to having fun? Take this quiz to find out!

1. How often do you do something that's just fun?

a) All the time. I'm almost always having fun (even if it means sometimes I ignore my homework or chores).

b) Occasionally. Sometimes I get too caught up in my responsibilities, but I'm trying to get better at enjoying myself.

c) Fun? Who has time for that?

2. Which activity sounds like the most fun to you?

a) Skipping school and doing whatever I want, all day long.

b) Watching my favorite movie after I finish my homework for the day.

c) Completing all the tasks on my to-do list.

3. Which adjective best describes you?

    a) FUN!!!

    b) Balanced

    c) Serious

If you answered . . .

Mostly As: You are definitely the life of the party—any party, anywhere. But don't forget that sometimes you have to buckle down and work hard, too. It's what Dolly would do!

Mostly Bs: You and Dolly are basically twins. Sometimes she gets too caught up in work, too, but she tries to find a balance between work and play that's just right.

Mostly Cs: You sound like Dolly in the early days of her career, when she worked herself so hard, she got sick. You gotta take a break for some fun or chill time once in a while—even Dolly does.

> *"Sometimes one of the great thrills is just to go ahead and do something nobody would expect me to do."*

You probably know this already, but having fun is a necessary part of life—and it's *totally* possible to balance it with dreaming big and working hard. Just look at Dolly! She's always known how to have fun, and even if she sometimes works *too* hard, she always seems to still find a way to have a grand ol' time.

You can have fun while you're working hard, and you can also have fun while you're taking time off. Dolly always makes time to go home to Tennessee for some rest and to take girls' trips with her five sisters or her BFF, Judy.

You're in charge of the fun in your own life. So go ahead . . . enjoy yourself!

Make a having-fun playlist to help get the good times started. Kick off the party with Dolly's song "Two Doors Down" and see where things go from there!

"Two Doors Down"

_____

_____

_____

_____

_____

_____

_____

_____

_____

_____

_____

_____

_____

Dolly PEP TALK!

Go ahead and make your own fun . . . with some wise words from Dolly giving you a fun-tastic boost:

"I make a point to appreciate all the little things in my life."

"I know some of the best Dolly Parton jokes. I made 'em up myself."

"Rhinestones, makeup, and hair are fun, but it's what's on the inside that makes you a truly special one."

"My life is fairly simple when I'm out of the limelight."

It's Time to Dazzle!

Now you all hopefully know a little—or a lot—more about what makes Dolly Parton so special, and how you can channel your inner Dolly to show the world just how special *you* are.

So go forth and shine, little rhinestones!
It's what Dolly would do!

Use the following pages to practice writing your own lyrics!

"Everything there is to know about me is in my music."

"*You have to be able to relate to the things you write about, but you don't have to live them personally.*"

"I'm a songwriter, so I have to live with my feelings on my sleeve."

"Songwriting is just as natural as breathing to me."

ABOUT DOLLY

Dolly Parton was born on January 19, 1946, one of twelve children, in the Great Smoky Mountains of Tennessee. Dolly's family was very poor, and Dolly often helped her parents take care of her younger siblings. The Parton family made their own entertainment and fun, and for Dolly that meant songwriting, singing, and performing from a very young age—starting with Knoxville radio and TV at age ten and an appearance on the Grand Ole Opry at age thirteen.

After graduating high school, Dolly moved to Nashville to pursue her music dreams. She released her debut album, *Hello, I'm Dolly,* in 1967, and since then she has sold over one hundred million records worldwide and has come to be a country, pop, and bluegrass music icon. She has appeared on and produced numerous TV shows, and she landed her first movie role, starring in *9 to 5,* in 1980 and has acted in many more movies since then!

Dolly has also written and published books; launched Dollywood, a beloved amusement park; and founded various charities to give back to her community and beyond. She and her husband, Carl, have been married for nearly sixty years, and they still make their home in Tennessee. ♥

Sources

Books

Kelley, True. *Who Is Dolly Parton?* New York: Penguin Workshop, 2014.

Marino, Lauren. *What Would Dolly Do?* New York: Grand Central Publishing, 2018.

Parton, Dolly. *Dream More: Celebrate the Dreamer in You.* New York: Riverhead Books, 2012.

Parton, Dolly, and Robert K. Oermann. *Dolly Parton, Songteller: My Life in Lyrics.* San Francisco: Chronicle Books, 2020.

Schmidt, Randy L., ed. *Dolly on Dolly: Interviews and Encounters with Dolly Parton.* Chicago: Chicago Review Press, 2018.

Smarsh, Sarah. *She Come By It Natural.* New York: Scribner, 2020.

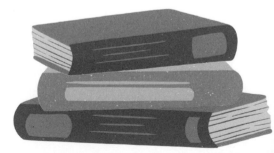

Websites

www.billboard.com/music/country/dolly-parton
-talks-50-years-in-nashville-and-supporting-gay
-fans-6296620

www.cnbc.com/2018/12/03/dolly-partons
-morning-routine.html

www.dollyparton.com

www.loc.gov

www.mentalfloss.com/article/68995/dollyisms
-26-quotes-and-quips-dolly-parton